IRIS APFEL

accidental icon

IRIS
APFEL

accidental icon

Musings of a
Geriatric Starlet

HARPER
DESIGN

An Imprint of HarperCollinsPublishers

FOR CARL

Dedicating this book to my darling Carl is one of the most difficult things I've ever had to do. How can one express the emotions, pleasures, and pains of sixty-eight years? Everyone he ever touched knows he was truly a Gentle Man. His humor and generosity were legendary. We did almost everything together. His encouragement and unwavering support made this book possible. He pushed me into the limelight and then basked in my success. He got much more of a kick from the accolades I received than I did.

I miss him madly. Sleep well, sweet prince.

AND FOR MY PARENTS

This might be unusual, but I couldn't go to press without a short ode to my parents. I adored Sam and Syd Barrel. They gave me life and this book that came with it. They provided me with both a super-solid foundation and an enormous passion for life. They were smart and strong, generous and funny. They were genuine world travelers, long before jet-setters existed.

Daddio was a pure nonconformist and didn't give a damn what anybody thought. He taught me to have the courage of my convictions. He instilled a sensible system of values and insisted I always read the right-hand side of a menu. He was the only person I ever knew who was intellectual and street-smart at the same time.

Mama was stunningly stylish. Her look was quite different from mine. Fashion-forward and original, she was decades ahead of her time in all areas. She was a university graduate and went to law school when most of the women of her day were relegated to the kitchen. Besides her many talents she was a crackerjack businesswoman.

It is only now at the end of writing this tome that I have come to the long overdue realization that my darling mother has indeed been my role model all these years.

CONTENTS

IN WONDER IT BEGINS...

INTRODUCTION

I NEVER EXPECTED

people to know
my name or recognize
my face.

I NEVER EXPECTED

to be called a fashion icon,

museums to exhibit my
clothing and accessories.

L'OFFICIEL

PARIS

N° 1009
Octobre
2016

...UTURE ET DE LA MODE DE PARIS

59

**ANS
DE
MODE
& DE
STYLE**

IRIS

Née en 1921
à New York

APFEL

Iris Apfel
en *Fendi*

HISTOIRES
DE
FEMMES DE
1 À 95 ANS

0 74470 72642 5   10 >

I NEVER EXPECTED

to be a cover girl or
the face of a cosmetics
company in my nineties.

to have a One of a Kind
Barbie doll made in my image.

I NEVER EXPECTED

to draw a crowd...

LET ALONE A MOB.

And I never expected to receive so many
flattering awards or honors—
by New York City at a ceremony at City
Hall and another in Harlem, and still
another by the city of St. Louis, where they

I NEVER EXPECTED

that anyone would want to make a documentary about my life, much less have it be nominated for an Emmy Award.

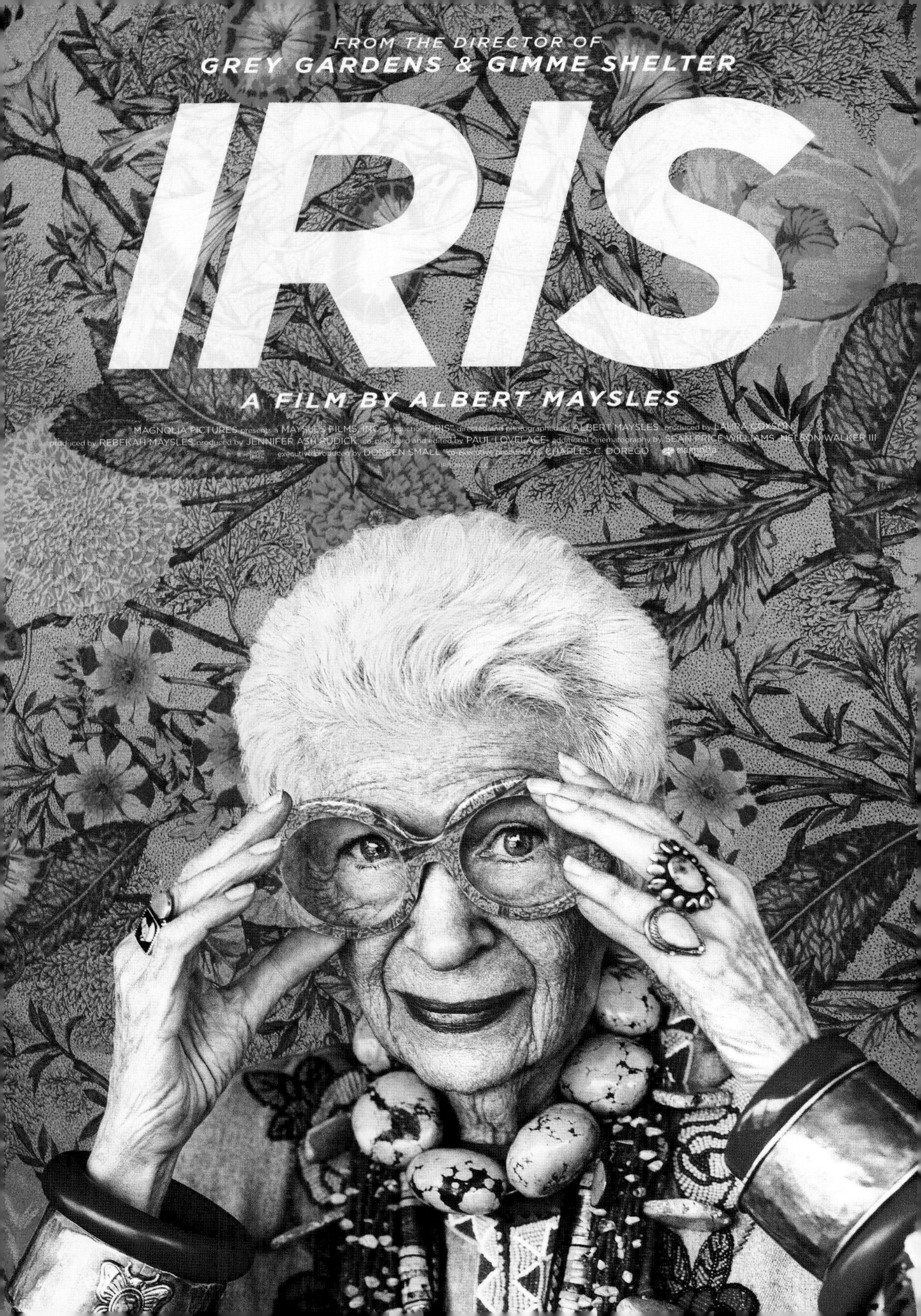
FROM THE DIRECTOR OF
GREY GARDENS & GIMME SHELTER
IRIS
A FILM BY ALBERT MAYSLES
MAGNOLIA PICTURES presents a MAYSLES FILMS, INC. production "IRIS" directed and photographed by ALBERT MAYSLES produced by LAURA COXSON
produced by REBEKAH MAYSLES produced by JENNIFER ASH RUDICK co-produced and edited by PAUL LOVELACE additional cinematography by SEAN PRICE WILLIAMS, NELSON WALKER III
executive produced by DOREEN SMALL co-executive produced by CHARLES C. DOREGO
magnolia

I NEVER EXPECTED TO WRITE THIS BOOK.

I never expect ANYTHING.

I just feel things in my gut and I do them.

If something sounds exciting and interesting,

I do it—and then I worry about it later.

Doing new things takes a lot of energy and strength.

It's very tiring to make things happen,

to learn how to master a skill, to push fears aside.

Most people would rather just go with the flow;

it's much easier. But it's not very interesting.

And as I always say,

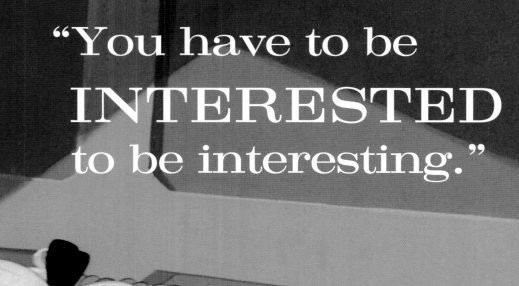

"You have to be INTERESTED to be interesting."

BELIEVE IT.

WHEN YOU GET OLDER, as I often paraphrase an old family friend, if you have two of anything, chances are one of them is going to hurt when you get up in the morning. But you have to get up and move beyond the pain. If you want to stay young, you have to think young.

Having a sense of wonder, a sense of humor, and a sense of curiosity—these are my tonic. They keep you young, childlike, open to new people and things, ready for another adventure.

I never want to be an old fuddy-duddy; I hold the self-proclaimed record for being the World's Oldest Living Teenager and I intend to keep it that way.

MUSINGS

A FAIRY-TALE BEGINNING... OF SORTS

WITH A RING-A-DING-DING-DING from the Metropolitan Museum of Art in early spring 2005, a new chapter in my life began. Harold Koda, then the curator-in-charge at the Costume Institute, was on the line, making me an offer I couldn't refuse. He wanted to do a small show of my fashion accessories and jewelry. The hitch was that it had to be completed within five months, or a nanosecond in the museum exhibition world, where shows are planned years in advance.

I agreed because I thought all I had to do was place my things in beautiful cases.

When Harold and the curatorial team visited me one morning to plan the show, he told me he had rethought the concept. To show accessories out of context didn't make sense, said he, for the public would like to see what accessories could do for an outfit. Then he asked whether I would be willing to supply at least five outfits to "use as a canvas." To be curatorially correct, he wanted to choose the outfits. My job would be to accessorize the mannequins as I would have accessorized myself sixty years ago or as I might wear them today with a new selection or a combination of the two.

"What do you have to show me?" he asked.

"What do you want to see?"

"Let me look, let me look."

Little did they know they had just opened Pandora's box. One closet led to another, and in the ensuing hours, we had peeked, pried, and pulled open every closet, every armoire, every drawer, every box, and every storage bin I owned. At one point, I even saw someone looking under the bed. Clothing seemed to gush from every direction. Things got so chaotic we finally had to buy ten pipe racks, push all the furniture aside in the apartment, and hang up all the possible candidates. By the end of the day, the surface had barely been scratched.

"We'll be back tomorrow, tomorrow, and tomorrow!" said Harold.

For several consecutive days after the selections were made, a truck arrived to pick up clothes. The final haul: about three hundred pieces plus hundreds of accessories. I'm sure if they'd had to pay for all that packing and shipping, they would've thought twice about how much they pulled! They were lucky I lived close by. In the end, the show exhibited more than eighty outfits and hundreds of accessories. I styled the mannequins myself.

When *Rara Avis* opened, I wasn't known internationally like I am now, but that changed quickly. The exhibit went from a small show to a big one . . . to a blockbuster. The Met didn't do any press-related material about me or display my photograph there. My nephew, Billy, went with different friends every weekend, then reported back with stories. He'd often hear people ask who I was. Once, he even

heard someone say that I was dead, which wasn't completely surprising, really, since this was the first time the Met had paid tribute to the style of a living woman who was not a fashion designer.

But when I heard that, I said, "Billy, do me a favor. The next time you hear somebody say that, just tap them on the shoulder and say, 'My auntie is alive and well. She's just walking around to save funeral expenses.'"

While the media coverage got the attention of a lot of fashion people, the real buzz began when my dear, dear friend, the late photographer and journalist Bill Cunningham, devoted his October 2, 2005, *New York Times* column On the Street to the show. He called it "In Her Image," and his enthusiasm for the exhibit—"You needn't fly to Europe to discover a marvelous, rare look at genuine style"—piqued everyone's curiosity. After that, people came in droves, and from then on, it was all word of mouth. In her review of the show, *New York Times* art critic Roberta Smith wrote, "Before multiculturalism was a word,

Mrs. Apfel was wearing it." I was stunned by the crowds and very flattered by the attention. I also figured once the show ended in January, that was going to be it. I'd be finished with the hoopla and go back to my old life.

But all of a sudden, people on the street knew me. I became cool to some—or hot—however you want to put it, yet I was no different than I was fifty years before. After the show opened, I was invited that fall to speak at New York University's fashion program. One designer got up and said, "Your show is wonderful. With it, you've given New York its loveliest Christmas present in years. And what has New York done for you?"

I blurted, "It's made me a geriatric starlet."

I'm not one for labels, but that one stuck and amuses me, perhaps because it's self-applied.

AFTER THE MET EXHIBIT CLOSED, I was contacted by other curators who had seen the show and wanted to bring it to their own museums. Soon enough, *Rara Avis* hit the road. It ran for three months at the Norton Museum of Art in West Palm Beach, Florida. The following year, it ran for four months at the Nassau County Museum of Art, in Roslyn Harbor, Long Island. But it really took flight in October 2009, when it opened at the Peabody Essex Museum in Salem, Massachusetts.

When the Norton came to me with the idea to do its own version of the exhibition, I was happy to oblige. And that wasn't because I have a home in Palm Beach—the experience of accessorizing the looks at the Met was so thrilling that I couldn't help but take the opportunity to do it again for a second iteration of the show, and again for a third. Whereas for the Met I only accessorized the

looks, at the Norton, Nassau, and Peabody I designed and mounted the shows. No, I wasn't lugging mannequins around, but the curators dressed them with my guidance. Not professional stylists themselves, they were happy to take my advice on where to place the mannequins, the clothes, and the accessories. I was really involved.

When I worked on the Peabody show, a curator there told me that my approach to dressing and accessorizing reminded her of improvisation—the basis of jazz. That made

> # "You needn't fly to Europe to discover a marvelous, rare look at genuine style."
>
> —Bill Cunningham, the *New York Times*, 2005

sense to me, as I've been a big jazz fan since I was a kid. I like to improvise. I like to jump in and do things that excite me without thinking about them excessively. I trust my instincts. I guess you could say I've lived a jazz life.

The Peabody will always hold a special place in my heart, not just because of its own excellent costume collection, but also because the curators there are now the custodians of my collection of accessories, clothes, and shoes. Every year since the show closed there, they have visited me and each time they come, we determine which pieces they are going to take with them back to the museum. Someday when I leave this earth, the Peabody Essex is going to have my full wardrobe—well, unless I change my mind.

SINCE THE SHOWS WRAPPED, I've had the opportunity to collaborate with a lot of wonderful creative pople. I don't have an agent or any person that is in charge. I don't have a website and I don't do social media, although I know people post pictures and drawings they've done of me.

Not only do I not do social media, I don't approve of it. What I eat, what I'm doing, where I'm going—that's nobody's business. And I have a rule: I don't do selfies—what better way to get sick than to have someone with a cold just stick their head up against yours and cough in your face?

At a dinner party several years ago, the host told me that she saw a photo on my Facebook page that caught her eye.

I said, "What's Facebook? I have no such thing!"

The "yes, you dos" and "no, I don'ts" went on for ten minutes, until she summoned a laptop. I took a close look at "my" Facebook page and there in the lower left-hand corner was a picture of my husband, Carl. Underneath, the caption read: "This is my darling husband, Joey." Well, I might not be the brightest candle on the cake, but I told my host that after sixty-some years of marriage, I thought I would know my husband's name. It was only then that she believed me.

I've been told that I have more than six hundred thousand followers on Instagram as of this writing, which is crazy, but I have nothing to do with it. People tell me "my" page is fairly well curated. It is run by a lovely young woman named Parisa, who lives in Vienna. We've spoken a couple of times since I learned of her handiwork, but I have no idea where she gets the pictures. Like I say, this woman is lovely, and I'm flattered that people have posted things about me, but I personally have no interest in doing it myself.

I don't give out my phone number, either, except to a select few, so nobody knows how to reach me. Somehow I still get calls from all over the world. They have found me through another source—through a museum, or by knowing someone who worked with me on a previous project, or from a mutual friend or someone else or something. People go through all kinds of shenanigans to find me, which is very nice, and it also lets me know they're serious about interviewing me or collaborating on some sort of project. By the time they get to me, though, they are usually very relieved and a bit grumpy because it's not like I've made it easy for them. But that's not on purpose; technologically, I live in the late seventeenth century. When people ask if they can send me an email, I say, "No darling. You can't do that. Send a pigeon. All I have is a quill and a candle."

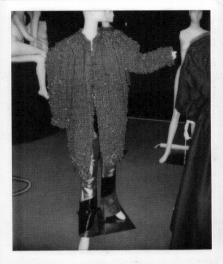

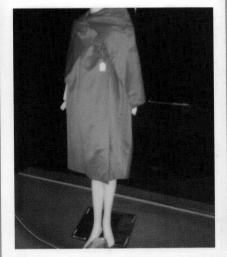

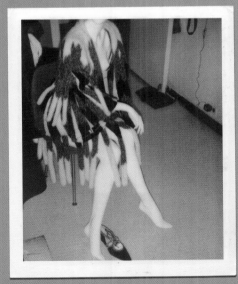

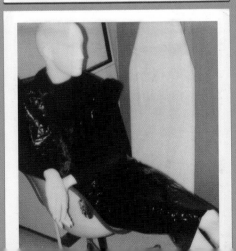

After *Rara Avis* opened at the Costume Institute at the Metropolitan Museum of Art, people kept telling me I was an overnight sensation.

"You're right," I would reply, "Except my overnight was seventy years!"

$**%!!!

WHAT

@**#

#**%**@!

EVER!

Although I'm in my 90s,
I still feel like I'm

5½

because I always look at
the world like I'm discovering
it for the first time.

If I could remain one age forever, I wouldn't. I don't believe in that.

But if I could do a little time travel, I'd like to be in one of Gertrude Stein's literary salons in Paris or attend a performance by the Ballets Russes, when Diaghilev was still staging the productions. I might like to stop in at the Harem in Istanbul during the eighteenth century. Then I'd stay right there but travel back to the sixth century, when it was still Constantinople, the capital of the Byzantine Empire.

BLACK-BELT
BEGINNINGS

I STARTED BUYING my own clothes when I was twelve. My mother—who always dressed beautifully and was extraordinary for her time in that she went to college and then law school but dropped out when she was pregnant with me—went back to work, opening a boutique during the Great Depression.

In spring 1933, Easter was coming and I had no new finery suitable for walking down Fifth Avenue in the Easter Parade. My mother was too busy working to accompany me—she felt truly sorry about that. But she did give me the magnificent sum of twenty-five dollars to go out and assemble an outfit by myself. I spent my first five cents on the subway ride from Astoria to Manhattan's S. Klein on the Square, probably the granddaddy of discount shopping and one of my mother's regular shopping spots.

I walked into the store and fell madly in love with a dress I saw on the first rack. I wanted to

"I buy clothing to WEAR IT, not collect it."

buy it very badly, but heeding Mama's advice to never buy the first thing I saw, but to comparison-shop instead, I headed for the department stores uptown, where I saw nothing I liked. Suddenly, it occurred to me that someone else might've bought my dress. I panicked and headed back downtown to S. Klein, where I embarked on a breathless search for my prize, which was no longer in its original location. I found it on another rack fairly quickly.

I grabbed it and gave thanks to God and $12.95 to the cashier. I then trucked down Fourteenth Street to A. S. Beck, the leading shoe emporium, where I selected a lovely pair of pumps for $3.95. That left enough money for a straw bonnet, a very light lunch, and five cents to get back home to Astoria.

My mother approved my fashion sense. My father praised my financial skill. Only my grandpa, who was an old-school master tailor, fussed and carried on about the button holes. All in all, it was a big success and the beginning of my career as a black-belt shopper.

I buy clothing to wear it, not collect it. I'm always asked about my "favorite" this or my "favorite" that. I hate that question! If I like something, I just like it. It's a gut feeling.

I didn't set out to build a wardrobe, either. I bought pieces when I found them—and when I could afford to buy them. I built my wardrobe slowly. I've been fortunate to have assembled a collection of couture pieces, beginning in the 1950s when I often traveled to Paris for my textile business. I'd go to the ateliers of the haute couture at the end of the season and ask whether there might be any runway pieces available for sale. I discovered the houses—Lanvin, Nina Ricci, Christian Dior, and Jean-Louis Scherrer, for example—who used mannequins with torsos similar in dimension to mine. I couldn't afford to have a one-of-a-kind piece made for me at a couturier. I also buy what I like: if a bracelet is fantastic and it's only five dollars, all the better.

European flea markets were also a favorite haunt, and I found a lot of great pieces—not the usual ready-to-wear. One day while shopping at one of my favorite textile stalls, I stumbled upon this eye-popping nineteenth-century chasuble in its original box. It had never been worn and was perfectly preserved. It was the typical outer vestment that a priest would wear during mass, except this

one had sleeves. It looked like a magnificent tunic: ruby-red silk Lyonnaise velvet with a whole panel of silk broché and a border of handcrafted passementerie. Beautiful.

I wanted to buy it, which made Carl hopping mad.

"Absolutely not!" he said.

I think he didn't want me to buy it because he believed people would think he couldn't afford to buy me regular clothes. We were about to have one of our rare combustions, when the good Lord sent the renowned fashion journalist Eugenia Sheppard our way. She saw the piece and swooned, "Oh, my. How gorgeous!" In the end she was much better and less expensive than a marriage counselor: Carl turned green and gave in.

I duplicated the fabric in our Old World Weavers line, and had pants and slippers made to complete the outfit. I never wore anything so much in my life, and I still have the outfit. Actually, I found a number of chasubles in France—all nineteenth-century, well preserved, and never worn. I started to collect them, which, I suppose, is one avenue to building a wardrobe.

I will admit that I should get my closets in better order. I have a lot of pieces, and they're all over the place—but who has time to organize? Certainly not me.

I just hang things up on pipe racks.

Most of the time I'm in such a rush that I can't find things. I'm on this shoot, I'm on that shoot, I'm traveling. I don't have time to unpack properly when I get home, and then I'm off again.

I'm often asked by my guests if they can see my closets, and I've had a hundred editors from big-time magazines ask if they can come over for a tour. That's never going to happen.

> You don't find out who you are unless you work at it.

ONE SIZE
DOESN'T
FIT ALL

I NEVER TRIED TO FIT IN. It's not that I went out of my way to be a rebel or do things that were not socially acceptable—unfortunately, I did have to learn how to play bridge when I was younger—but I learned early on that I have to be my own person to be content. If you try to be all things to all people, you end up being "nothin' to nobody."

The way I dress may be "different" or "eccentric" to some who feel the need to label, but that's of no concern to me.

I don't dress to be stared at; I dress for myself. When you don't dress like everyone else, you don't have to think like everyone else.

Here's the critical part: I know I'm not an island, but rather part of the main, to paraphrase Mr. John Donne. I fit in, but in my way. I have never been much of a conformist on any front, actually, and it hasn't hurt me yet in my ninety-some years, so I think I've been doing something right.

Somehow, I learned about the importance of fitting in very early in life. When I was six, my parents sent me off to summer camp in upstate New York for two months. I was the new kid and I learned very quickly not to voice my opinion too strongly in a group. I can't remember what happened, but I must have seen something that someone did backfire on them. Whatever it was, I learned that if you make a point of bonding with the group and they accept you, they will actually like it when you do something original.

But if you don't try to be part of things, forget it. That's when your originality is going to work against you. Fit in first and then step out. There is a difference between being perceived as original and being accepted, even loved for it, and being perceived as different and resented for it. You can have your cake and eat it, too.

MOTHER
KNOWS BEST

WHEN I WAS ABOUT four years old, my parents and I went on a summer vacation at a resort. My mother loved dressing me up for the various events of the day, pulling together ensembles for swimming, lunch, dinner, and whatever happened to be going on in between. As she dressed me and made her final adjustments to my outfit, she would stand me on an orange crate she must've found somewhere on the premises.

One night during this ritual, as I was later told, I began to scream, howling my head off, which led to all these people running into our room to see what sort of abuse my parents were doling out. I was shrieking like I was being attacked by a madman with an ax. Yet fellow guests and resort staff found me alive and well and dressed beautifully, as usual.

"It doesn't match! It doesn't match! It doesn't match! It doesn't match! It doesn't match! It doesn't match!"

My mother had put a ribbon in my hair that didn't match the rest of the outfit, and I just went bananas.

Later I realized, as usual, that Mama knows best, because now I hate matchy-matchy. But I didn't know any better then.

I don't
like a
minimalist
look for
myself.
I like stuff;
I like being
surrounded
by a lot of
things that
give me
pleasure
to look at.

MORE IS MORE

AND LESS IS A BORE.

STYLE VERSUS FASHION

FASHION CAN BE BOUGHT.
STYLE ONE MUST POSSESS.

—EDNA WOOLMAN CHASE

Editor in Chief, *Vogue*, 1914–1952

That says it all. And that's why I say:
You can **LEARN** to be fashionable.
You can **BECOME** fashionable.

But as for style...

EITHER YOU GOT IT or YOU AIN'T.

STYLE IS IN YOUR DNA

I'M CONSTANTLY ASKED for style advice. I hate to give guidelines because what works for one person is not necessarily going to work for another. But here's what I believe. The worst fashion faux pas is looking in the mirror and seeing somebody else.

You have to
KNOW YOURSELF
before you can find your own style.

If I tell you what to do, it's not your style anymore. It's mine. Your style has to come from you. Style cannot be bought or learned—it's in your DNA. You can get help to bring it out; you can learn how to be better dressed, but in the end, style is inherent. A personal shopper or stylist can't give it to you, either.

Style is
ATTITUDE, ATTITUDE, ATTITUDE.

Style is not about wearing expensive clothes. You can have all kinds of money and have no style at all. You can be dressed in the latest couture, shod in ten-thousand-dollar shoes and be baubled to the nines, and look like a Christmas tree.

It's not what you wear but
HOW YOU WEAR IT.

I'm just as happy to wear bangles that cost me three dollars as I am to wear valuable pieces—and I like to mix high and low, putting things together to wear as the spirit moves me. When you try too hard to have style, you look uncomfortable, like you're wearing a costume, like the clothes are entering the room before you do. If you're uptight, you won't be able to carry off even a seemingly perfect outfit. If that's happening, I say abandon the whole thing. It's better to be happy than well dressed.

My mother worshipped at the altar of the accessory.

I GUESS I INHERITED THE BUG.

SHE TAUGHT ME a simple but invaluable lesson. She always said that if you invest in a few well-made classic pieces in good fabrics—like a little black dress—and put your money into accessories, you'll have a million different outfits.

I've always followed that advice, perhaps to what some people might consider an extreme, but I dress for myself so I've never given other people's opinions a second thought.

YOUNG LADIES DON'T WEAR JEANS

I WAS ONE OF THE FIRST women to wear jeans. I love denim and have never tired of wearing it. When I was in college in Wisconsin in 1940, women couldn't buy jeans like they can now. Jeans were not a fashion item. They were only sold in stores that carried work clothes for men sized like Paul Bunyan. You couldn't buy smaller sizes, and certainly not anything that would fit me.

Nonetheless, I was wholly dedicated to the pursuit of indigo; I had a vision of little old *moi* in a checkered cotton turban, oversize gold earrings, and a crisp white shirt, anchored by a pair of classic work jeans that I couldn't get out of my head. I entered the local army-navy store and inquired about said item. My inquiry was met with a strange look, both quizzical and dismayed. If I recall correctly, I may have even detected a whiff of disgust.

"Don't you know? Young ladies *don't* wear jeans."

I didn't care if young ladies didn't wear jeans—I wanted those jeans.

I begged the shopkeeper to help me. He kept saying that they had nothing. I asked him to size down a pair for me. To no avail. He did everything but kick me out.

I went back the following week, and we repeated the routine. And I went back again the week after that. I did this for several weeks. I was Little Girl Blue, but I was determined to triumph.

One day, the shopkeeper either came around and pitied me or decided he couldn't bear the sight of me again, so he mail-ordered a pair of boys' jeans for me. When I got the call, I was delirious with joy, visions of my ensemble to come dancing in my head.

FROM THE DESK OF

IRIS APFEL

TO: THE READER   FROM: IRIS APFEL

SUBJECT: THOUGHTS ON LIVING AND DRESSING

If you're not risking, you're not living.
It never hurts to take a risk, to try
something new.

You only fail if you do not try.

I never thought that I couldn't do something
because I was a woman. I wanted to start a fabric
business, so I just figured out how to do it. If
I had thought about opening Old World Weavers too
much, I probably would have thought only of the
pitfalls and then I probably wouldn't have pursued
my dream. Sometimes you just have to take action,
even if it's a small step.

In my ninety-some years of walking planet Earth,
I have applied this philosophy to living—and
dressing—and it has never steered me wrong.

Dress for YOURSELF.

Listen to your inner muse and take a chance.

Why not wear something that says,
"HERE I AM TODAY!"

Besides, if you make a mistake, it's okay. It's
just clothes.The fashion police are not going to
come and haul you off to jail.

ADDENDUM

TO: THE READER   FROM: IRIS APFEL

SUBJECT: FURTHER THOUGHTS ON LIVING AND DRESSING

Be curious.

Have a sense of humor.

Have a sense of wonder.

Think before you speak.
You are never sorry
for the things you don't say.

And don't procrastinate!

Iris Apfel keeps the front row guessing.

IMPROVISATION

AFTER I FINISHED COLLEGE, I thought I'd try my hand in fashion journalism. The year I graduated, I was in contention to work for *Vogue* in Paris as part of the magazine's Prix de Paris contest, but the offices closed during World War II. Determined to become a fashion editor, I took a sub-entry-level job trafficking copy at *Women's Wear Daily* on Twelfth Street in New York City. It paid fifteen dollars a week—a paltry sum to say the least, even in those days. This was well before the age of hypertechnology, of course, and pneumatic tubes were few on the premises, so with the latest stories in my hot little hand, I would run up and down the stairs, from department to department, delivering the news to one editor after another. I ended up learning nothing about the fashion business, but I did get into the best shape of my life.

After several months, it became apparent that I'd get nowhere in the establishment, as ninety-eight percent of the editors were too old to get pregnant and too young to retire. I moved on, landing a plush gig working for Robert Goodman, the eminent men's fashion illustrator of the day. Ensconced in very swanky digs in a penthouse across from Saks Fifth Avenue, he had many illustrious clients, and I began to meet new people, including interior decorator

Elinor Johnson. Elinor was involved with Jack Heinz (and his "57 Varieties"), and he bankrolled her decorating forays into luxury old-world apartments near Grand Central Terminal, like the Louis Sherry, the Marguery, and other beautiful buildings. She'd buy some apartments and take long leases on others, then decorate each one for an imaginary tenant, a particular person she'd craft in great detail, just like a Method actor. She was a Method decorator. Lee Strasberg would've loved her.

Elinor couldn't decorate a paper bag, but she put together a crackerjack team of interior designers, all of whom were either on their way up or down the ladder. She brought me onboard because she said she believed my career was on an upward trajectory. On one occasion, we were working on an apartment that needed a coffee table. But there was no furniture delivery, as we were in the middle of World War II. So we went down to the Bowery and found old columns and had the capitals cut off, which we took with us. We also picked up a stunning piece of thick glass. Once back in the space, we put the glass on the capitals,

and voila! We had a cocktail table. That particular piece came together through improvisation alone.

But it wasn't long before I took up the pen again. As fate would have it, by doing so I was able to parlay a stint as a reporter at Grossinger's—the iconic Borscht Belt resort in Ferndale, New York—into my earliest work as an interior designer.

Founded in 1914 by Austrian immigrants Asher and Malke Grossinger, the hotel published a daily newspaper. Its mimeographed sheets covered happenings at what was becoming a sprawling destination. Grossinger's was known not only for its top-rate entertainment—performers included Sammy Davis Jr., Milton Berle, and Shecky Greene, to name a few—but also for its VIP guests, who delighted in the many social engagements, strictly kosher menu, and sports facilities. It was the glory days, when no one could travel because of the war. Everybody was there.

Graduation from the University of Wisconsin was still in my not-too-distant past, and I knew the Grossingers, who knew I was interested in writing. They asked me if I'd like

to fill in for a reporter who was taking a month's leave from the paper.

Upon arrival, I was shown my digs in the help's quarters. Not such glamorous accommodations, but I hit the ground running: I covered virtually all the events taking place at the resort. I interviewed guests, reporting on their experiences. People love to see their name in the paper. My efforts were rewarded when the family moved me into a little apartment on the top floor of the beautiful house they lived in on the property.

I needed a lot of clothes for the job—for breakfast, lunch, and dinner and for everything in between. There was a story to be found 24/7. My deft assemblage of these little numbers resulted in compliments and I

became known for putting together a good look or two. This was very flattering, as I didn't have a lot of money, let alone a clothing allowance from the resort, so I had to mix and match. But guests took notice, and it was through those conversations I'd let slip my interest and experience in interior design, which in turn, led to work.

Since I didn't have a body of work or references, guests must have figured that if I could put together an outfit, I could probably do the same for a room. Suddenly people looking to renovate the interiors of their homes approached me to do the job, with seemingly inherent faith that I could. I got some very good clients this way and decided to start a business.

"My clients didn't have run-of-the-mill taste which suited me just fine..."

My clients didn't have run-of-the-mill taste, which suited me just fine, as I don't believe that one style fits all, anyway. I would find out as much as I could about their interests, style, and taste, and if they couldn't articulate these things, I riffed off of what I did know about them in every applicable sense to create an interior that expressed their aesthetic. Then there were those who didn't like working with me because I never drew up designs of what I was planning to create for them; I just dove right in. Sometimes it was difficult, especially when clients were very rigid about what they wanted. With most of them, though, I would eventually get carte blanche—or at least partial carte blanche—to design their interiors as I saw fit. I was left to improvise, which suited me just fine. All roads lead back to jazz.

LOVE AND MARRIAGE

I WAS MARRIED for sixty-eight years. That is a long time to be together. Sometimes it felt like a century, sometimes it felt like a nanosecond. We had a wonderful relationship; the hows, whys, and whens of it are too private and painful for me to relay at the moment, having recently lost my darling.

I met Carl Apfel very briefly while I was on a vacation at Lake George. A few weeks later, I had lunch at the Plaza with my mother and an old beau who was the buyer of haute couture for Neiman Marcus in Dallas. As he walked me back to my office that afternoon, we passed by Bonwit Teller on Fifth Avenue. We stopped for a while to talk about what caught our eye in the window.

That night, as I came home, the phone was ringing off the hook. It was Carl.

"I loved the hat you were wearing today," he said. Then he went on to compliment my wonderful suit, my bag, my shoes—the whole outfit. Then he asked me out.

I couldn't figure it out at first, but then he explained he had been stuck on a bus that had broken down on Fifth Avenue in front of Bonwit Teller at the time I happened to be standing there.

We had a whirlwind courtship.

We had our first date on Columbus Day.

We got engaged on Thanksgiving Day.

I got blinged on Christmas Day.

We were married on Washington's birthday, February 22, 1948. I wore a strapless, pink lace dress. I sketched it, and a woman—a couturier whom my mother used to make special things—made the dress. It was fitted with a full skirt, and it had a little cape, which I wore for the wedding. I kept it to wear on formal occasions. I thought spending a lot of money on a wedding dress only to wear it once and put it in a box was pretty impractical.

We were married at the Waldorf Astoria. The ceremony was held there, with cocktails and dinner. It was a small affair, 120 people, but it was beautiful. And it was a pink wedding—I couldn't have the decor clash with my dress!

Palm Beach Hotel
THE BRILL MANAGEMENT
PALM BEACH FLORIDA

January
23rd
1948

Dear Mr. Apfel,

Thank you very much for your letter of January
20th and for the reservation it contains, pur-
suant to your previous conversation with our
New York office of that date. We are pleased
indeed that you will be with us at the Palm
Beach Hotel.

Upon your arrival here with Mrs. Apfel on Wed-
nesday, February 25th, for a stay of three full
weeks, you will find awaiting you a twin studio-
bedded room with private bath, at the rate of
$36.00 per day for the room for two until March
10th, and $26.00 per day thereafter for the room
for two persons.

Your deposit check of $100.00 is hereby acknow-
ledged; this amount will be credited to your
account at the end of your stay, as above.

We look forward to the pleasure of your company,
and assure you and Mrs. Apfel a hearty welcome
and a most enjoyable stay.

Most sincerely,

PALM B...

MS:JG

Mr. C. B...

The
WALDORF
ASTORIA
NEW YORK
☆
CLOSE COVER BEFORE STRIKING MATCH

THURSDAY, MARCH 11, 1948

Carl Apfel
Returns From
Honeymoon

Mr. and Mrs. Carl B. Apfel of
Forest Hills are making their home
here following their honeymoon in
Palm Beach. Mrs. Apfel is the
former Iris Barrel.

Chaplain L. Goldberg performed
the marriage ceremony in the Hotel Waldorf-Astoria. A reception
for 120 followed at the hotel.

The bride was gowned in cloud
pink lace with a capelet enbroid-
ered with tiny matching heads
and a bonnet type veil of matching lace and illusion. Her nosegay
of pink lipped white orchids was
surrounded by various pink flowers.

Mrs. Clifford Shuman was the
matron of honor and Dr. Everett
Apfel was his brother's best man.
The ushers were Charles Taubman,
Arthur Waxman, Morton Diamond,
Jack Meyers, Daniel Myerson, Clif-
ford Schuman, Joseph Fishman
and Leward Werbein.

Mrs. Apfel is the daughter of
Mr. and Mrs. Samuel Barrel of
Astoria. She was graduated from
the University of Wisconsin and
attended Cornell University.

Her husband is the son of Mr.
and Mrs. Harold Apfel of 68-38
Yellowstone Boulevard. He is a
graduate of the New York University School of Advertising.

Queens TB Assn.

THE SECRETS OF
A LONG and HAPPY MARRIAGE

PEOPLE ALWAYS ASK ME what the secrets of a long and happy marriage are. I don't know the secrets, but here are some things that come to mind.

1 I list this first because it's always what I seem to say first whenever anyone asks: have a sense of humor because that will get you through bad times and make good ones even better.

2 Respect each other.

3 Give each other space; don't get in each other's face all the time.

4 Accept that you won't always agree, but trying to stay more or less on the same wavelength is very productive.

5 Don't sacrifice who you are. And accept who your partner is. You may be a couple, but you are not one person.

6 Don't be petty. Most couples fight about stupid little things that they've blown out of proportion. And there's nothing more annoying than nit-picking.

7 Have a sense of adventure; do new things together.

8 Accept that you won't always like the same things and people.

9 If you like to do something and your partner doesn't, do your thing anyway! And once in a while, also do the thing your partner loves to do that you don't.

10 Be creative. Sharing new interests keeps a relationship fresh.

ALADDIN'S CAVE

MY INTERIOR DESIGN BUSINESS was booming, and I was on my way to see a new client in Brooklyn. Her travel instructions left a great deal to be desired; to begin with, I got off at the wrong subway stop and walked straight into an unexpected rainstorm.

I was frantically trying to figure out where I was when I spied what I thought had to be a mirage: a long, slender store window with a beautiful Tiffany glass screen at one end, against which was draped an outfit by the great Norman Norell. I swooned and gasped. At the other end of the window was a mannequin magnificently dressed in Pauline Trigère.

Waterlogged and anxious, I entered the emporium, a cavernous room filled with clothing on pipe racks, women in various stages of undress scrambling about, and dozens of disgruntled husbands yapping at their wives to step on it.

I realized I had stumbled upon Loehmann's, the legendary discount retailer. I snooped around the racks, saw nothing that pleased me, and wondered what all the fuss was about. I was about to leave, when another customer came to my rescue. She explained that I was in the low-end department and that if I were to go to the back of the store and walk up a flight of stairs, I would come to the exalted "back room." I followed her instructions and fell into Aladdin's cave: clothes by all the great fashion designers were hanging there in dizzying array.

The clothes were gorgeous, and the prices were incredibly low. I was dripping and drooling all at once. I had found the Holy Grail, but had neither the time nor the money on hand at that point, so I thanked the Lord for my good fortune and promised myself a return trip.

I quickly became a regular. Every time I went back to Brooklyn, I would stop by and pick up a few more pieces. Often, I had no time to try anything on as I was always running to meet a client. The store had a no-return policy then, but that never deterred me because, being a fabric freak, I figured I could always turn an oversize dress into some gorgeous pillows. The textiles were truly to die for!

Occasionally, Mrs. Loehmann would sit on a high stool on the selling floor to observe all that went on. A petite woman, she wore her hair in a topknot. She was always dressed in a high-button blouse, a long drawstring skirt, and high-button shoes—and she always carried her miser's bag full of cash from bailing out the garmentos on Seventh Avenue. She reminded me of a character in a Toulouse-Lautrec painting.

She often fixated on me as I sashayed about. One day, she summoned me over.

"I've been watching you, young lady," said she. "You're certainly no beauty, but you've got something much better—you have STYLE!"

I didn't quite understand what she meant at the time, but her comment was a precursor of much to come.

When I was a little girl, I asked my father what
he was going to give me for my birthday.
He replied, "Why should I give you anything?"
"Because it is my birthday," I stammered.
He retaliated, "I don't have to give you anything.
You had nothing to do with being born!"

%***#$!

WHAT

CONCENTRATION
SIX NOT-SO-EASY PIECES

PEOPLE OFTEN ASK ME about the genesis of my passion for fabric. For a long time, I couldn't pinpoint a moment. But then one day I had a flashback to my early childhood—and all was revealed.

I was an only child and for many years the only grandchild on both sides of my family. This meant I often attended family events that kids didn't go to. We lived in Queens, and periodically, my parents would take me to my father's parents' home in Brooklyn, where all the aunts and uncles would gather for a social evening. For the first ten or fifteen minutes, everyone would pet me, pinch my cheek, and ask me questions. Then they'd get bored with me and go and have a drink or play cards; I'd be left standing there like a little fool.

My grandmother realized she had to do something to keep me entertained. She was a very charitable woman who did a lot of work for the poor and the sick. In those days, she was one of the founders of a hospital and an old-age home. She also had four daughters; they were always sewing for charity.

One time, when I was still very young, she took me to a back hallway where there were two big closets, and said, "Sit on the floor. I'm going to give you a treat."

I obeyed. She opened the closet doors, and out tumbled several huge white sacks that had been stuffed inside. She opened one bag, and then another, and what I saw made my eyes pop: a gigantic bunch of little fabric remnants in all sorts of colors and patterns—there were scraps of all kinds, of all shapes and sizes.

Then she said, "Here, sit on the floor and play with them. Do whatever you want. If you're good, you can take six pieces with you when you go home."

I was fascinated, and this became the routine whenever I went to visit. I would sit on the floor in the back hall and put combinations together. If I didn't like a setup, I'd "fix" it. I clearly remember agonizing over a change, especially if I thought I wanted to pull a swatch from one of my "finished" arrangements to put into another, newer one, because then it meant I'd have to fix that, too. Obsessed with texture, color, and pattern, I spent whole evenings entertaining myself this way. Time always passed too quickly, and I was always sad to leave when my grandmother came to fetch me. Looking back, it's very clear playing this way honed my eye and gave me a very deep interest in fabric.

THE DUKE
TO THE RESCUE

I'VE BEEN A JAZZ BUFF for as long as I can remember. When I was in high school, I had two classmates who used to work for an advertising agency that sponsored the 1930s NBC radio program *Let's Dance*. Benny Goodman's band was a big part of the show—and he was all the rage. These boys made themselves a pile of money because they took a bunch of tickets they were supposed to send out to the sponsors and the sponsors' friends and they kept them to sell instead. We all bought the tickets because we were all dying to hear Benny Goodman play. There was a whole contingent of us from William Cullen Bryant High School in Long Island City, who went every week to hear him. We used to go crazy. We used to dance in the aisles in our saddle shoes. It was really fun.

When I was in college, I transferred from New York University to the University of Wisconsin at Madison, and I found myself painfully shy of a few credits that were lost in the transfer, credits I needed to fulfill my curriculum and graduate.

I had read the course selections backward and forward, trying to find something interesting that I hadn't already taken at NYU. To make a long story short, I found a course called Museum Administrations I.

My first task was to find the professor and the building where the class was held. It was no easy matter. The building was way across campus and no classes were held there. When I finally located the room, I knocked on the door, and was told to enter by a very surprised, tiny, elderly gentleman. He wanted to know why I was there; it seemed I was the very first creature to sign up for his class in eight years! He had all but given up hope for students, patiently waiting to retire instead. When I asked what the course was about, he said whatever I wanted it to be. And somewhere in all of that, he explained his yearning to found a museum of indigenous American culture.

"What about something on jazz?" said I.

"Brilliant!" said he.

"What should I do?" I asked.

"What about writing a paper?"

"Brilliant!" I retorted and merrily skipped off to the library only to be stonewalled again. There was not one word written on the subject to be found there.

After agonizing over my problem for weeks, as well as the notion of spending the rest of my life on campus, a piece of good fortune came my way. I read in the newspaper that Duke Ellington and his band were coming to town to play at a local movie theater between film showings.

Aha! I thought to myself, *I will go to the source.*

I put on gray flannel trousers, a gray cashmere sweater, a Cornell blazer—a stunning white flannel jacket with burgundy piping and beautiful buttons that an old beau had given to me—and a great pair of loafers and headed down to the theater instead of my usual classes.

I snuck backstage and knocked on the dressing-room door. Ray Nance, a violinist in the band, opened the door, and looked me over.

"Lordy, lordy, who's your tailor? What can we do for you?"

"The Duke was charming, and to this day is still one of the most charming men I've ever met. He was suave, sophisticated, and elegant."

He invited me in and upon hearing my mission, told me to wait for the Duke to finish his set.

When the Duke came back to the dressing room, I was bowled over. He was charming, and to this day is still one of the most charming men I've ever met. He was suave, sophisticated, and elegant. We spent the rest of that afternoon together; the Duke regaled me with jazz tales galore. He told me that his band was going to be in Madison for the week and that I could come back whenever I wanted to. He gave me loads of information: We talked about different musicians, their work, their style. We talked about different movements within the jazz genre. The fact that he took so much time to speak with me was extraordinary. Needless to say, my classroom seats were empty that week.

At the end of the seven days, the Duke announced that he and his band were planning to take the milk train to Chicago's South Side, where they would play at a theater for two weeks. All the jazz greats and his friends who were anywhere in the area were going to stop by. He told me he'd be delighted if I would come, and he'd introduce me to them all. That was just about the most wonderful thing I'd ever heard.

On the last night, the band never went back to the hotel. In 1940, Madison was the most awful place when it came to race. African-American people had to stay in a rathole of a hotel. When Paul Robeson, the actor and great singer, came to town, the college set up a bed at the student hall for him because the hotel was so terrible. So I understood what was meant when band members said they were going to wait for the milk train after the last show.

That last night, we were walking down the street when street cleaning began. Billy Strayhorn, a great with the Ellington organization—but also a depressive—was very drunk. He started throwing all of his sheet music into the street, where it literally began going down the drains. We all ran around, trying to catch the pages. A lot of it just perished.

I had to clear a hurdle to get to Chicago—my mother. She had to grant permission for me to leave the sorority house where I was living. PERMISSION DENIED.

I chose to go anyway. In Chicago, I met the musicians Duke told me about. Not only did they come to watch him play, they sat in with him for some great live jam sessions. And I was able to speak with them for my paper. Problem solved.

MATISSE ET MOI

WHEN THE TATE MODERN curators created the exhibition *Henri Matisse: The Cut-Outs* in 2014, they asked me to do a video that would be part of the show. They wanted me to talk about the similarities between Matisse's work and the way I dress. Honestly, I had never thought about that before—but I thought it would be fun, and when I started to choose clothing for the shoot, I realized that it was true. A number of my clothes look very . . . Matisse-y.

For the video, I was filmed paging through the show catalog and talking about the pieces from my closet that I thought complemented the cutouts. One cutout I chose, *The Snail*, appealed to me because of its subdued, yet brightly colored squares. Their tonality allows them to blend beautifully. If the work were a piece of clothing, it would be a great example of color blocking. So I put together a color-blocked outfit: I wore vivid multicolored bracelets and a colorful multi-tiered necklace along with a bright-orange vintage cape. That floor-length cape with a high, curving collar was also as heavy as a horse blanket, but as I said at the time, "We have to suffer for our art."

The Horse, the Rider and the Clown, with its intense color, brought to mind a white Gianni Versace trouser-and-jacket combination. And as a self-professed jazz freak, I was delighted to discover that the work comes from his *Jazz* portfolio. I'm so happy to have a love of music and color in common with Monsieur Matisse.

When Matisse made this work, he was ill and could no longer sculpt, yet in the catalog he is described as carving through color. What a wonderful image. I like to imagine him thinking of his scissors as a sculpting tool, carving through color blocks or maybe, like a scythe, cutting through huge fields of magnificent color.

Above: **Henri Matisse,** *The Snail,* 1953

COLOR

CAN RAISE
THE DEAD.

ON COLOR
A PERSONAL MANIFESTO

Personally, I can't live without **COLOR**.

In the proper tonality,
I've never met a **COLOR** I didn't like.

I've always said that the world
today is so gray that we need
COLOR more than ever.

COLOR is a living, breathing thing.

And let's face it, life can be dull;
you might as well have a little fun
with **COLOR** when you dress.

I wear red lipstick

because I like it and I think it's becoming on me. Matisse once said, "A thimbleful of red is redder than a bucketful," and Man Ray likened wearing red lipstick to the "dash and dignity of a courageous heart," which sums it up perfectly. Red lipstick is minimal in its simplicity and elegance, but maximal in its impact, power, and glamour. If Minimal and Maximal had a baby, it would be the perfect red lipstick.

DONALD

Whatever happened

to mystery and glamour

and all that
good stuff?

YOUR
SMARTPHONE
IS NOT
YOUR BRAIN

IF YOU DON'T use your legs, you won't be able to walk. If you don't use your brain, you won't be able to do anything. This whole technology obsession is giving rise to a generation of zombies. But it's not just that—people aren't connecting with one another. People go out on a date: they sit across from each other, and instead of talking, they're texting.

Technology is wonderful for medicine, for engineering, for all those kinds of things. But on a human level, it's disastrous. People use smartphones and computers as a crutch. Technology has ruined a whole generation of young people. It has robbed kids of their childhood. They have become button pressers. They think if they press a button, they're very curious. That's not curiosity or imagination—that's just access to a world created for them.

So many basic human capabilities have gone out the window. The three Rs—reading, writing, and 'rithmetic—aren't enforced in school, either, so young people can't read, write, or add two and two. No one's developing memory, because their phones remember and do everything for them. I'm fairly good at remembering telephone numbers, which I always thought was a pretty common skill, but today it seems to stun people almost every time I make call.

My mother died in 1998, four weeks after her hundredth birthday. From about the time

Carl and I were married to not so long before she died—about fifty years—he would give her an adding machine every year, and she would always send it back.

He would say, "Why do you do that? I'm trying to help you."

And she'd say, "No, it's no help. If I use an adding machine, I'll lose it. I won't be able to add anymore."

She could do really big, big sums in her head well into her later years.

At first, everyone said I was an old fogy when I proffered my thoughts on the subject. But now there are "phone-free" get-togethers at which people have to give up their phone for the course of a meal and "tech-free" times when families go cold turkey on tech for an evening or, God forbid, a whole day.

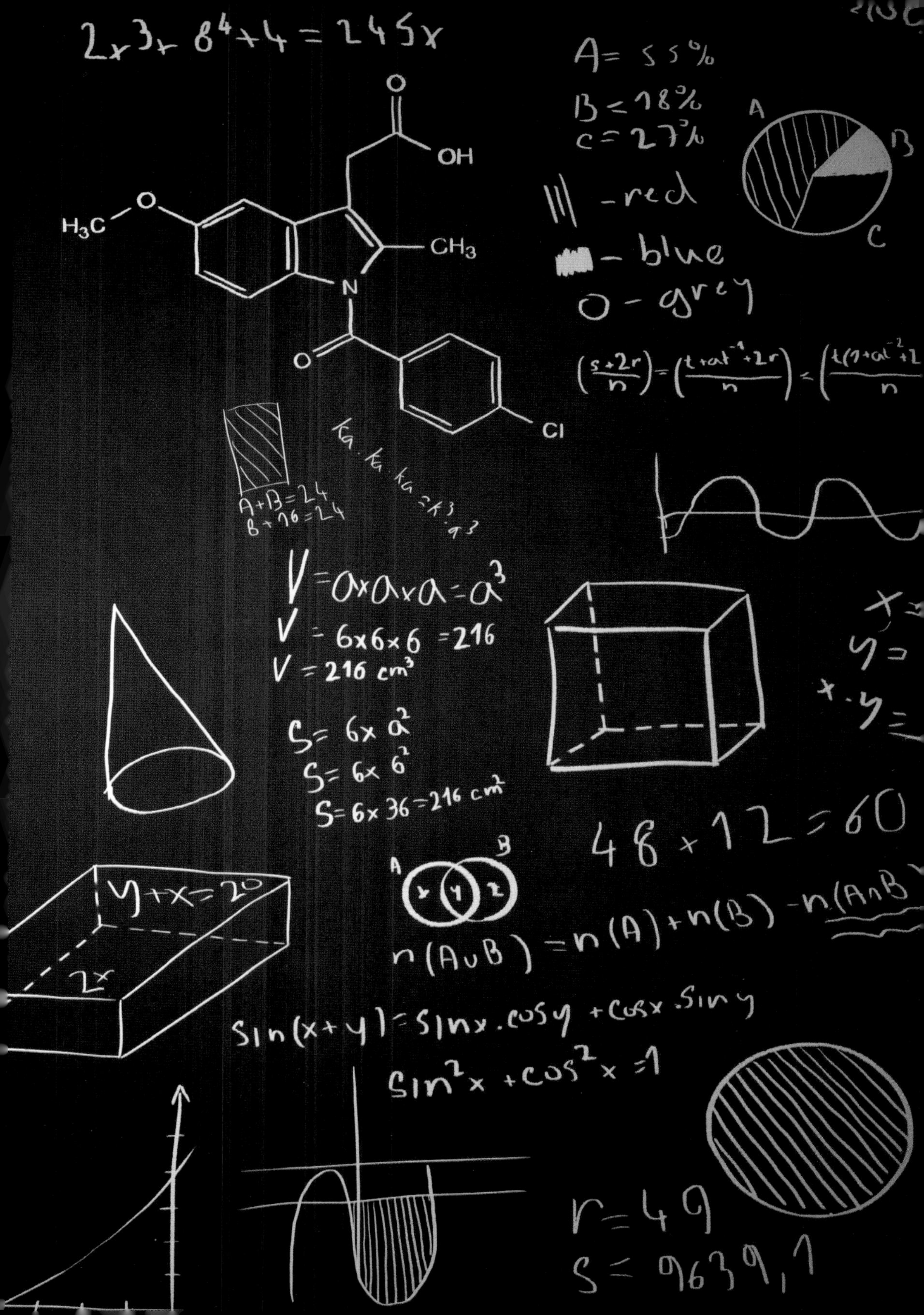

$$2x3 + 8^4 + 4 = 245x$$

$A = 55\%$

$B < 78\%$

$C = 27\%$

||| — red

▓ — blue

○ — grey

$$\left(\frac{s+2r}{n}\right) = \left(\frac{t+at^{-1}+2r}{n}\right) = \left(\frac{t(1+at^{-2}+1}{n}\right)$$

H_3C

CH_3

N

O

OH

Cl

$k_a \cdot k_a \cdot k_a \leq k_3$

$A + B = 24$

$B + 76 = 24$

$V = a \times a \times a = a^3$

$V = 6 \times 6 \times 6 = 216$

$V = 216\ cm^3$

$S = 6 \times a^2$

$S = 6 \times 6^2$

$S = 6 \times 36 = 216\ cm^2$

$$46 + 12 = 60$$

$y + x = 20$

$2x$

A $\bigcirc$ B

x y z

$n(A \cup B) = n(A) + n(B) - n(A \cap B)$

$Sin(x+y) = Sinx \cdot cosy + cosx \cdot Siny$

$Sin^2 x + cos^2 x = 1$

$r = 49$

$S = 9639,7$

THE FAME GAME

THE CULT OF CELEBRITY (a word I hate), is a sad commentary on our society. It's almost like as fast as technology evolves, the human race devolves. Reality shows are dreadful and allow people to live in someone else's image. You can turn on your phone and follow a famous person's life almost to the extent that you are living it. Whatever happened to the cultivation of an inner self? It's painful and it's work, but it always pays off.

The obsession with the superficial reminds me of all the young ladies I went to school with who were pretty—the girls who had perfect hair, the ones who dated the football players, the prom queens. Because they were pretty, they relied totally on their looks to get along. And they didn't grow in any other way, unlike girls who looked like me, who realized they had to develop themselves in other ways to get along in the world.

To be known and admired for giving something to the planet or helping people is one thing, but for me, that's where the intrigue with fame ends. Being famous just for being famous is ridiculous; it doesn't make a person memorable or interesting. I've met celebrities and have forgotten them just as fast as hello because they had nothing much to say. There are a lot of people who are memorable to me for any number of reasons—humor, intelligence, the way they always tell a good story—and it doesn't matter to me if anyone else knows who they are.

Privacy is a precious commodity and when you're famous, it becomes elusive. And if you start looking outside yourself for validation, you're really in trouble.

I didn't look for recognition. People come to me to do projects and if what they're asking me to do is new or sounds fun or creative, I'm in. It's all about the work for me. I like to work, to do new things. If people are interested in my style, amused by my candor, or amazed by the fact that I'm still out there hoofing it in my mid-nineties, that's great, but I never had any intention of becoming a role model on aging. I believe we are put on this earth to do something. If you stop using your brain at any age, it is going to atrophy and eventually stop working. It's harder when you get older, but you just have to do it. Why curl up in a ball and wait to die?

I've become increasingly recognized in the years since *Rara Avis*, through the press and all that. But *Iris*, the documentary Albert Maysles made about me, pushed the public recognition into another sphere altogether when it was released in 2015. At first, I wasn't going to do it; I didn't really want a film crew dragging around behind me, and I couldn't really see what would be so intriguing about my life, if you want to know the truth. But eventually, my very good friend, Linda Fargo, one of New York City's leading lights in fashion, convinced me I'd be a fool not to do it, and I let Albert in, because even though I only met him at the beginning of the film, we just hit it off. He never got in my hair and we filmed on and off for four years. While the film is about me and shopping and style and all that, it's become more significant to me for another reason. Many people have told me that they see *Iris* as a love story about Carl and me. And it is. But really, it is a dual love story—a story of my love and passion for Carl and for my work.

I was shocked when Albert passed away in March, just a month before *Iris* was released; he had never let on that he was sick while we were working together. A few months later, Carl died just days before his 101st birthday. I'm glad, now that he's gone, that we did the film; it was about passion on many levels, and that's what's important to me.

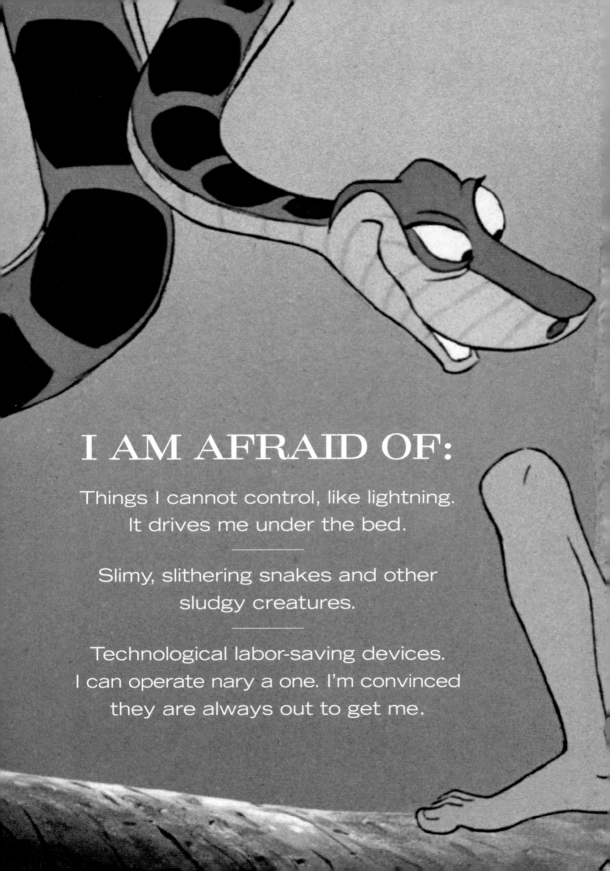

I AM AFRAID OF:

Things I cannot control, like lightning.
It drives me under the bed.

———

Slimy, slithering snakes and other
sludgy creatures.

———

Technological labor-saving devices.
I can operate nary a one. I'm convinced
they are always out to get me.

OPTICALLY SPEAKING

PEOPLE ALWAYS ASK me how many pairs I have of the oversized glasses that I wear. Honestly, I don't count them. I probably have three or four pairs that I wear all the time and a few others for special outfits.

I've loved looking for junk at flea markets ever since I was a kid. And for some reason, unusual spectacle frames have always fascinated me. Whenever I saw unique ones, I would buy them and put them in an old shoebox of my mother's that I kept in my closet.

Once in a while, I'd take them out and try them on. They were so much fun. I didn't need glasses then, but sometimes I'd just wear the frames without the lenses because I thought they were a great fashion accessory.

Many years later, when I was much older and truly needed them, I thought, *Well, if I'm going to have to wear glasses, I might as well have GLASSES.* So I took out the biggest pair I had, and I had lenses put into them.

Why do I wear such large glasses?

The bigger to see you with, my dear.

Anyway, you have to have fun.
If you can't have fun,
you might as well be dead.

NICE WORK IF
YOU CAN GET IT

BY THE LATE 1940s, my interior-decorating business had taken off. One day, while working on this beautiful home on Long Island, I was looking for fabric, well, to be exact, a vision of a fabric I had conjured up in my head—but I was sure it had to exist in a showroom in New York City. I wanted that fabric and I couldn't find it. It didn't exist. I was going absolutely mad.

As luck would have it, I ran into a young woman I had gone to school with. She was working for a fabric wholesaler, so I asked her if she knew where I might find the fabric I imagined. She said she didn't know, but if I wanted something special, perhaps I might want to go see her father. As it turned out, her father was reputed to be a textile genius. He had come

to America from southern Italy with a few handlooms and set them up in Paterson, New Jersey, where he sold the wondrous fabrics he produced. Eventually, he opened a little mill in Long Island City and worked for fabric wholesalers like Scalamandré, Lee Jofa, and Schumacher.

I went to see Papa and told him about the fabric I was after. He told me to come back with the design I was talking about, and if he liked it, he'd make it. He had the ability to make a few yards of a fabric at a time, too, which was a real advantage; most people wouldn't make such a small quantity of something special because it's so expensive. He brought to fruition the fabric of my dreams, and it was a big success. Not long after, he asked me if I had any more designs, and we began to make some textiles together. I used them for my business and he sold them, too.

One day, he brought up the idea of going into business together: he'd run the mill, I'd do the designing, and Carl would sell and handle the business end of things. Carl and I thought it was a good idea, but we were concerned about how we were going to do it. We didn't have a load of money. We needed to make a living. At the time, Carl was in business with his father.

We decided we would test the market first. In those days, interior designers were mostly staffed professional businesses, not an individual with some helping hands, like it is today. We made a few samples, and Carl made appointments with designers during his lunch hour. The response was positive, so we made more and more samples.

Finally, we had so many samples that we had to put them in a suitcase, but it quickly filled up and became so heavy that Carl couldn't carry it. So he put wheels on it—he

was the first one to do that. If he had patented that roll-along suitcase invention maybe we wouldn't have had to do anything else for the rest of our lives. But whenever I said that, he always responded, "Don't worry—think of all the fun we would have missed."

We had many, many samples because every time Papa did an order, he'd take a piece and give it to me. One day, the suitcase was nearing the brink: bulging with samples, it was almost impossible to close, especially because one of the main fillers was a heavy antique taffeta with satin backing. That's when I had the idea to make a color blanket. I took all the samples to the mill, laid them out, and graded them, using about twelve inches of each color so they looked harmonious.

One day after months of trying, we finally got an appointment with Dorothy Draper, the doyenne of decorators at the time. The morning of the meeting, as luck would have it, that special blanket sample came in from the mill. Carl threw the blanket on the top of the other fabrics in his suitcase and set off.

When Carl was ushered in to meet with Mrs. Draper, a very large woman, she was standing behind an enormous trestle table, which she used as a desk.

She looked at Carl and said, "Well, young man, what have you got to show me?"

He opened the suitcase and with a great, dramatic flourish, threw the sample blanket across the table.

She gasped and said, "Oh my God, you know, this is the first intelligently scaled stripe I have ever seen."

She thought it was a striped fabric. Well, Carl didn't have the heart to tell her it wasn't. She wanted to order three hundred yards.

The next day, we had a visit from Sara Fredericks. She sold beautiful designer clothes in her shops in New York, Boston, and Palm Beach—and she was well known for her impeccable taste and love of luxury. Sara had heard of us through an antiques dealer we both knew and she called to ask if she could come to our apartment after business hours. In the end, she placed an order for 250 yards of another design. We figured if these decorating and fashion mavens thought we were good enough for them, we should give going into business a crack.

We opened Old World Weavers in 1950.

In those days, it was very difficult to get into our part of the fabric business, so we had to be inventive. Eventually our persistence paid off. We began by doing small custom work for clients. We made everything to order because we couldn't afford to hold any inventory. One job led to another, and things worked out beautifully for the first couple of years. But as labor unions entered fabric production, it became more difficult to do small quantities affordably.

It was time to switch gears.

In 1953, we traveled to Europe to see if we could find special fabrics to replicate. When I want something, I'm relentless, so we went absolutely everywhere. We found brochés, brocades, brocatelles—all kinds of wonderful hand-woven creations. Not only did we look for special fabrics, but we also needed to find the mills that had the ability to replicate them authentically.

A lot of manufacturers we wanted to meet with would literally shut the door in our faces

because we weren't looking for large-enough quantities; what we needed amounted to sample sizes as far as they were concerned. To make matters worse, French war hero Captain Roger E. Brunschwig was already in business with the bulk of the mills in France. But we were persistent, and we finally got our foot in the door. We then tried our luck in Italy, where we had great success.

I liked to say our collection of fabrics was the most dazzling one going. Eventually, we began to travel to Europe twice a year, simply because there were fabrics there that we couldn't get elsewhere.

We specialized in replicating as closely as possible fabrics from the seventeenth, eighteenth, and nineteenth centuries. I never did an adaptation; I always tried to make designs that looked old and different. That's what led us all over the world: Sometimes we met with museum curators who would open the doors to their collections to help us find what we were looking for. After finding old documents that supported my designs, I would search out the mill that would be able to produce it.

I learned how to spot the right textiles at markets by doing. I don't think you can learn how to do it from a book. It takes practice, and I believe in apprenticing and honing your eye. It's hard work and it takes years. It's like being a good cook who doesn't work from a recipe but who just knows what ingredients to put in. Anyway, there's no free lunch. That's what I learned.

Eventually, we opened a showroom on the top floor of a four-story walkup, a townhouse at 115 East Fifty-Seventh Street in Manhattan, right in the heart of the prime antiques district. Socialites would find out about us and come to the showroom, a space that was styled like a French salon; shortly thereafter, they started sending their decorators our way. We worked with top designers, decorators, and architects with a very prestigious clientele including Greta Garbo, Estée Lauder, Montgomery Clift, Marjorie Merriweather Post, and Joan Rivers, just to mention a few of the boldface names who started coming to our townhouse. We showed samples out of an armoire, but when got bigger, we displayed our wares on racks. That spoiled the salon look, but it also meant that business was booming. I couldn't argue with that.

SHOOT FROM THE HIP

THERE ARE SO MANY THINGS I loved about Carl that if I were to list them all, they wouldn't fit in these pages. He was hysterically funny. He had the most delicious, offbeat sense of humor. We used to laugh a lot.

When Carl and I ran Old World Weavers, I used to make clothes for myself using sample lengths of fabric. After a few years, I decided to do something for him, so I had a bunch of spiffy pants made out of our upholstery, too. Some pants were sporty, wild prints, while others were formal and elegant, suitable for gala events. People would admire his trousers, invariably asking where he got them.

He always replied, "I just shot my couch."

He was always good at shooting from the hip.

At one point, we created fabric and passementerie for Marjorie Merriweather Post for the redecoration of Hillwood, her magnificent estate just outside of Washington, D.C.

One morning, the telephone rang.

"This is Marjorie Merriweather Post," the caller said. "And I need to speak to Mr. Apfel immediately about the fabric I have just received." I asked her to hold on and, trembling, I summoned Carl to the phone.

"Mr. Apfel," she said. "I am in my salon sitting at the top of an eighteen-foot ladder with

a ruler in my hand. I am admiring the window treatments that were installed last evening. The fabric is marvelous; and I just love the festoons and trimmings. Tell me," she went on, "these little decorative bits that go across the top—how many should I expect to have in a running yard?"

Carl took a deep breath, then spoke.

"Mrs. Post," he said. "Every morning I eat Post Raisin Bran. Can you tell me how many raisins I am supposed to have per tablespoon?"

"Touché, Mr. Apfel," she said. "Now I better get down before I break my neck."

Everyone tells me that I am a
BLACK-BELT SHOPPER.
I like to say I was born with
a souk sense.

I LOVE FLEA MARKETS and open-air markets—oh, I just love markets. Period.

In a former life, I must have been a hunter-gatherer. I like any place where I can forage. I like the thrill of the hunt, the unexpected. I love digging through bins and finding things. There's just a certain excitement that grabs me, a feeling of energy and mystery because I never know what I'm going to find—that's what I find so exhilarating.

Haggling is half the fun of it. You have to feel people out: some merchants will haggle and some won't, regardless of the culture of the market. But in most cases, if you're told a tunic costs one hundred dollars, and you are foolish enough not to try for a better price, you've just ruined the merchant's day because he feels he made a mistake not to ask you for double.

Although I don't shop too much anymore, I'm still an avid jewelry collector.

I don't get any great pleasure if somebody just comes and presents something to me. If I had a sugar daddy who told me to go to the most expensive store in the world and splurge until my heart burst, it would be a sad day. I wouldn't have any fun at all. I'd find a lot of lovely things, but the thrill wouldn't be there. I like to dig and scratch. It's the process that turns me on.

THE WHITE HOUSE YEARS

104—White House, Washington, D. C.

DURING THE TIME Carl and I owned Old World Weavers, from 1950 to 1992, we participated in many design restoration projects, including work at the White House for nine presidential administrations, from Harry S. Truman through Bill Clinton. Because of our work there, people would sometimes refer to me as the "First Lady of Fabric" or "Our Lady of the Cloth," which amused me.

People always ask me what it was like decorating the White House.

Let me tell you: we didn't decorate the White House, and neither did Jacqueline Kennedy or any of the other first ladies, for that matter, because historically accurate restoration is the driving force behind any changes to the building or its furnishings.

That's the rule.

We didn't come in and say: "We don't like the scale of this; it should be reduced" or "We don't like this color; we should change it to that color."

We didn't work for the presidential administrations, either; we worked for the U.S. Commission of Fine Arts, re-creating the antique fabrics as close to the original as humanly possible. The commission reviews all designs proposed for new or restored government buildings, among other things.

We did our best to make the main floor of the White House exactly as it was when the original furniture was introduced. Whatever we were re-covering, we had to make absolutely sure that everything we touched was historically accurate.

We also did work on the second floor, in the private quarters where the First Family lives. There are no rules there; they can decorate that space—bedrooms, guest bedrooms, private sitting rooms—the way they want to.

Most of the presidents and first ladies weren't terribly interested in restoration or decoration at all, except for Pat Nixon, who was passionately interested in everything we did, even though she knew nothing about the finer points of historical restoration. She often would ask if she could accompany Edward Vasson Jones, the interior architect for the White House at the time, when he came to visit us. Mr. Jones made all the necessary decisions on the refurbishing.

We let Mrs. Nixon pick out the fabric samples she liked, and she'd take them back to Washington with her. Invariably, she'd call the next day and say sheepishly, "Mrs. Apfel, as usual, I selected the wrong thing. Please choose what's correct and come to Washington on Thursday for lunch." In the end, we always knew that Mr. Jones would make the right choices; we never had the heart to correct Mrs. Nixon because she was such a lovely lady.

THE LANGUAGE OF FABRIC

MY FIRST TRIP TO ITALY was to Naples. I found it very unusual. It had a tinge of Africa about it—it's a great melting pot of boisterous, outgoing people.

About an hour or so to the north, there's a city called Caserta. It became a silk center when the Bourbon kings arrived and set up a palace. They brought craftspeople with them to produce their fabrics and in the process established a group of very high-end silk mills.

The first mill we went to hired an interpreter because we didn't speak a word of Italian and the fellow in charge there didn't speak a word of English. The interpreter was a funny little man, very short with graying red hair parted in the middle; he wore eyeglasses with very small lenses, which reminded me of Benjamin Franklin. For some reason, he had a cucumber in his pocket. Every time he thought nobody was looking, he took a bite of the cucumber.

There we learned that the language of fabric is not in the dictionary, as our interpreter spent the whole time looking—I can still see him licking his finger and turning the pages—for words that weren't there. But not speaking the native language turned out not to matter because we were on the same wavelength as the mill owner. We didn't need language; we understood each other—and fabric.

All the same, I knew I had to learn Italian or else doing business would be almost impossible. Since I had no time to go to school, I learned by listening very intently. I put words and actions together. I bought some Italian children's books, like *Pinocchio*. I developed an enormous vocabulary, but knew no grammar. I speak Italian only in the first person and in the present tense. This way of thinking taught me something very important: to be present, to live in the now. If people ask me if I speak Italian, I say, "Yes, with courage and no verbs."

I've found that speaking well doesn't matter. If you are open and have a sense of humor about the way in which you're communicating, people can read your expressions and body language to get a sense of what you are about.

Actions speak louder than words.

Le avventure di Pinocchio

di C. Collodi

DISEGNI A COLORI
DI ATTILIO MUSSINO

R. BEMPORAD
& FIGLIO
EDITORI - FIRENZE
MILANO-ROMA-PISA-NAPOLI

AROUND THE WORLD IN EIGHTY YEARS

DOLPHINS SWAM BESIDE US and jumped out of the water as if to greet us, as my father and I sailed up the Bosphorus and into Istanbul for the first time. It was dawn. The sky was azure and clear; there was not a television antenna in sight. When I returned just a few years later with Carl, it was another story—the pollution was terrible and the sky was filled with wires.

In Paris in 1952, if you weren't seated for dinner by seven thirty, you didn't eat. Now if you come in before nine o'clock, everyone looks at you like you have two heads. It's my conviction that dining later and later is a sign of a degenerating society.

Traveling makes life rich. And I like a good adventure. I've never gone anyplace where I wasn't working; actually, I don't like to go to a resort and just sit there. I never have. I don't know what I would do with myself. Carl and I traveled all the time for our business. We went all over Europe, to Paris and London numerous times, and I think we covered every square inch of Italy. We made many acquaintances through work, so we learned about great markets and who had the best of everything. We discovered things by just walking everywhere. Wandering down little streets, you stumble into things, whether it's a tiny shop that carries incredible buttons of all colors and shapes or a local lacemaker. That's how I became familiar with these cities and where to shop, and that's how I decorated my home and built my collections.

Amo l'Italia! And if you've never been, I'd say see as much of Italy as possible. That Rome is still standing is extraordinary. I love that there are piazzas everywhere you turn; that you can come around a corner and find yourself in front of the Pantheon; and that there are still grand palaces like the Doria Pamphilj, with its courtyard and orange trees, sitting just off the Via del Corso. I'll never forget the trulli—circular drystone buildings in ancient Apulia; there are no other buildings like that anywhere in the world.

Venice is like being in a strange, decadent dream—the Moorish architecture; the striped pilons with their peeling paint, which the gondolas are tied to; the water slapping against the buildings; the tiny alleys that always feel a bit wet. I like that little hint of exotic—it stirs my bones.

That's why I loved Istanbul, too, with its bazaars of all kinds and old-world culture: it's beautiful, sophisticated, and gritty. Once we ended up in Bursa, home of the Turkish towel, on a Sunday and there was nothing to do, so we decided to go to one of the baths. I was a bit obsessed with the gold-colored tin they give you for your soap and wash cloth, so I bought one—and still carry it as a handbag today. And I'll never forget the sight of all the ladies sitting around the edge of the pools—without a stitch on and crocheting baskets.

Tunisia is special. In the markets there, you buy silver jewelry by weight; artisanship and beauty have nothing to do with the price, which always amused me. I loved Sidi Bou Said, a tiny town on a steep cliff, just outside of Tunis. It's like an itty-bitty version of Capri. All the houses are white with azure doors and trimming, and there are cobblestone streets, and lots of flowers everywhere. On one visit, the mayor's daughter was getting married in the town square late one night, and we were lucky enough to be invited to the wedding. It seemed like the whole village was there, crowded into the plaza or watching from above, leaning out from their balconies. The whole affair lasted until dawn. They sure knew how to throw a party.

"I like that little hint of exotic— it stirs my bones."

We walked into a lot of experiences like that. In Morocco, we were driving around and stopped to admire a white horse adorned in silver as part of a rural wedding procession. We couldn't speak a word of Arabic, but the people were so friendly. They invited us to the wedding party—and we went.

Something similar happened when we were driving in Crete. We noticed a large number of cloths spread out along an embankment with grapes drying on them—we got out to look. The people drying the fruit had been watching us. They tried communicating, and the next thing we knew, they were pulling us up the embankment for an outdoor lunch under the Cypress trees.

In 1958, we were touring around the Irish countryside and came upon a cluster of houses with the most charming thatched roofs. I was dying to photograph one of them, but Carl thought it would be rude to do that without asking the owners. So we chose the house with the fattest roof and rang the bell. Out came two elderly gentlemen who readily gave us permission. It was tea time, and the kettle in the antique walk-in fireplace was bubbling. They insisted we stay for a cup. They were delightful.

In Lebanon, we would go to the Baalbeck International Festival, the oldest cultural event in the Middle East, every year. There was this man who'd come every year too, to sell coffee. And it was the worst coffee you can imagine. But he had this gorgeous brass table on which he'd set four smashing brass urns in graduated sizes for the coffee. As the coffee brewed down to the perfect muck, he'd dump the dregs of one urn into another. This went on until there was one urn left filled with coffee that just kept getting stronger and more horrible as it emptied out. But everyone would drink it, and we drank it too, mostly to continue our annual conversation with the proprietor about buying his brass table and urns. And one year, we prevailed—I always wondered whether he was ready to retire or whether we had put him out of business.

Beirut had an incredible casino and a wonderful gold market. In the 1970s, we became friendly with this funny little Russian man at one of the markets. Every time we visited, he'd invite us into his office, where he had all this gorgeous Chinese jewelry that he had brought back from his travels. He loved to drink, and the more he imbibed, the cheaper his wares became. It was ridiculous. Beirut was beautiful, though; it really was the Paris of the Middle East.

Speaking of Paris, who doesn't love
PARIS?

Giriat

Everyone should go to Paris.

BARCELONA, by the way, is not to be missed for the tapas, tapas, tapas, and vino.

I love the little winding streets filled with shops, all the incredible greenery, and the silver jewelry. And of course, for the work of the architect Antoni Gaudí, a fellow lover of color and the unusual.

And then there's Hong Kong, with its supercharged energy, expats from around the world, and new buildings that scrape the sky. The overlay of Western ideas on old Chinese culture is inescapable—you feel it everywhere.

I'll never forget London, though. I love the old traditions of London Town. And every day there is another market to go to somewhere. The shops, the museums, the parks, the flowers—they never fail to knock me out. Next to New York, it is the most multilevel city going.

Rio was a study in contrasts. Looking down from the terrace of the luxurious, thirty-odd-room villa where we stayed to the unbelievably abject poverty of the favela below was an emotional experience I could have lived without.

I found Mexico City to be super sophisticated. There, I was particularly enchanted with the architecture, not only the sleek twenty-first-century skyscrapers, but also the townhouses built in the style of Louis XV and Louis XVI during the era of Emperor Maximilian and set on streets that remind me of Paris's loveliest. I went bananas over the homestead of Frida Kahlo and Diego Rivera. Their palette was staggering. Brilliant, bold, saturated colors were everywhere.

LET THEM EAT CAKE

ITALY WAS ALWAYS a favorite. We visited Siena during *Il Palio*, which is held twice a year when the city's seventeen *contrade* (districts) each enter a horse in the medieval race in the Piazza del Campo. There's a lot of pageantry and celebration around the event, and each contrada has a social club that holds a banquet the night

before. During our stay, I had become friendly with our inn's majordomo, who invited me to be his guest at his contrada's banquet.

For dessert, they served a *torta della nonna* (grandmother's cake). It's prepared however Grandma sees fit, but this one was filled with *crema pasticcera* (custard) and topped with pine nuts and powdered sugar. The crust was made of *pasta frolla* (shortbread pastry). It was so divine that I told the majordomo I wished I could get cake like that in the States.

He took me to meet the head baker, who was overjoyed that I liked his confection so much and presented me with the recipe, folded neatly into an envelope.

Later that evening, when I got back to the hotel, I opened the envelope and began to read the recipe ingredients: Four hundred eggs, sixty pounds of flour—honestly, I don't remember the numbers exactly, but they were outrageous. I started to laugh hysterically: the recipe he had given me was for a cake that would feed the whole contrada.

YOU CAN'T GO HOME AGAIN.

If an experience was

WONDERFUL,

don't try to re-create it.

It will never be as

BEAUTIFUL

as it was the first time.

WHERE IS THE HOUSE OF THY FATHER?

The morning of August 4, 1958 found Carl and me on the deck of the S.S. *Coronia*, waiting to disembark. It was Carl's birthday, and we were headed for Dublin's antique row—Grafton Street—to buy him a present.

Carl was mad for watches. I'd never seen a man with so many watches, everything from the crummiest reproduction to the most expensive Breitling. It was crazy—and he never knew what time it was.

He owned nary a piece of jewelry, though, and I planned to remedy this after he begrudgingly agreed to accept an unusual ring. We went from shop to shop where we found rings of great historical significance and staggering beauty, but nothing with pizzazz.

Before we took the trip, our Manhattan townhouse was broken into and my collection of silver was stolen. They were connoisseur crooks; they took only the best silver, all eighteenth-century Irish silver and Georgian pieces. They took the best liquor. Posing as laundrymen, they made sure to take the furniture cushions with them to complete the ruse, all the while smoking Havana cigars. So, while ring shopping, we decided to replace the stolen silver. We found a store that was a treasure trove—we found our silver and some other things. We had everything set aside and went off to have lunch.

We ate at a pub, trying every Irish brew known to man and talking to people around us. We met a young Irishman who had just returned from Israel, where he served as a Freedom Fighter in the Six-Day War. He offered us a ride back to the ship, with a stop at the antique dealer's first. He professed to have a lorry waiting outside at the ready; Carl and I had visions of grandeur, only to be directed to a broken-down wreck left over from World War I. After a puttering, stuttering ride, we arrived at the antiquarian and stumbled out of the lorry, much to the chagrin of the elegant doorman standing outside. We were three sheets to the wind.

The shopkeeper, a very ample gentleman, greeted us from behind the counter. On his very large hand, he wore a very unusual ring. It was shaped like a lion in the form of a throne chair.

"THAT'S IT!"
I screeched.

"THAT'S
THE RING!"

The gentleman was taken aback and explained that it was the ring of the Wandering Jew which bore the inscription, "Where Is the House of Thy Father?" He had just purchased this extraordinary piece at the auction of King Farouk's prized possessions on behalf of the lord mayor of Dublin as a gift for the chief rabbi of Jerusalem, an important Irishman who had come home for a visit to much fanfare.

He said the ring was not for sale.

DEFINITELY NOT FOR SALE.

I refused to take no for an answer. I threatened not buy any of the silver I'd set aside. I've never done anything so nasty in my life—before or since—but I was hell-bent on getting my prize.

The shopkeeper finally capitulated and allowed Carl to try on the ring.

THE RING WAS TOO BIG AND IMMEDIATELY FELL TO THE FLOOR WITH A GREAT THUD.

The shopkeeper saw his chance, and offered to size it and send it to New York along with the acquired silver. I was drunk, but I wasn't drunk enough to buy that line.

"Thank you very much," I said, "but I will take it now and have it sized in New York." Triumphant, I departed with the ring.

I gave Carl a beautiful birthday party that night. We were all having a fine time, when suddenly a fellow passenger came along and started telling everybody about the ring. Unbeknownst to us, he had been elsewhere in the shop and witnessed the whole gruesome episode. Everyone wanted to see the ring, so I went down to the cabin to get it. As I came back, they were wheeling out the birthday cake. It was midnight; everybody was dancing and drinking. Carl put the ring on his finger. We didn't think about it anymore until we got to the cabin at 4 A.M. Strangely, the ring, which had been much too large hours before, was still on his finger.

Carl tried to take off the ring, but he couldn't. Together, we tried to pull it off, but it would not budge. He was on the verge of panic; he thought not being able to get the ring off meant that he was now under an Egyptian curse, as this was the ring of the Wandering Jew. Finally, we decided to wake up the ship's doctor to help us. Groggy and in his bathrobe, the doctor stumbled into our cabin, took one look at Carl, and pronounced his diagnosis and remedy: he told Carl that he'd had one too many and to sleep it off. He was sure Carl would find the ring on the floor in the morning.

Well, that didn't happen.

THE RING REMAINED ON FOR MORE THAN FIFTY YEARS.

Carl even had several hand surgeries, and the doctors couldn't remove it. A couple days before he died, the ring fell off. He put it back on, and it stayed on, but really, it was too loose. When he passed away, the ring fell off again.

When I look back on it, I can see how the whole ring thing might seem crazy. I never wanted to talk about it, I was sure people would think I was nuts or that I was making up a story. But, whether you believe it or not, it happened.

I still have the ring. I'm keeping it for myself.

SUCCESS

If you're happy, have found love, are
surrounded by good people, doing what
you like, and giving back to others,
that's **SUCCESS**. Selling your soul
for a buck is not worth the real
price you pay—not to me, anyway.

REGRETS

I haven't done everything properly.
No one has or does.
While I may have a few **REGRETS**,
I don't dwell on them. If I did,
I'd be in a booby hatch.

If your hair is done properly and you're wearing good shoes,

you can get away with ANYTHING.

YES, I SAID THIS. And yes, I meant it, but let me qualify my point: you can get away with "anything" within the context of dressing appropriately for your age and the occasion.

That's another lesson I learned from Mama, who was always dressed impeccably. Everything was always in its place—from her hair to her shoes. She had her own style, but she always looked *poifect*.

The word *appropriate* seems to have disappeared from the current lexicon—in both the way we dress and act. I remember strolling down Fifth Avenue in the 1950s and 1960s with great pleasure. Everybody looked put-together and crisp. Now when you walk down the street, especially in the summer, you just want to throw up. People are not getting dressed anymore. Everybody looks

like a mess, like they're on their way to a shower bath or who knows where. Flip-flops, sweatpants, leggings instead of trousers, jeans that are twelve sizes too tight, short shorts that expose way too much—they should all just be outlawed. And when you add the accessory du jour, the cell phone, the impropriety is even worse—people have less and less respect for those around them. And don't even get me started on those selfie sticks. I say invest in a mirror instead and use it.

It's upsetting, because when style and good manners go away, the whole culture seems to disintegrate.

Good hair and shoes count for a lot, but they don't give you license for a sartorial free-for-all in between.

MIND YOUR PEAS & Q'S

I DON'T like BROCCOLI RABE,
BRUSSELS SPROUTS, or WATERMELON.
I LOATHE CUCUMBER.
Do not put it on my plate. If cucumber touches anything,
I CAN'T EAT IT.

I SHOULD HATE carrots and spinach. When I was four years old, my dark hair coiffed à la Buster Brown, I lusted for blond curls. One day I confided my secret to a friend of my mother's. She in turn told me that if I insisted that my mother feed me carrots and spinach every night that I would soon have a head of luxurious golden ringlets. I did as she advised, driving my poor mother over the rails, as she soon became weary coming up with new spins on spinach and cultivating carrot concoctions. After three months of stuffing myself nightly as such, my locks were status quo. It was then that I realized that my mother's friend must have been a vegetarian witch. I also probably became the youngest cynic on record.

M·A·C AND ME

MY FIRST BIG JOB in beauty and fashion came when I was at the tender age of ninety. M·A·C Cosmetics called me and asked if I was interested in developing a limited-edition line for winter 2011.

I don't do any project unless I can be very involved. I like to roll up my sleeves and actually work on it. I created the seventeen-item line, including lipstick, lip liner, eye shadow, face powder, and nail polish. Usually in these collaborations the company will give you a selection of colors and only want a simple response of whether you like it or not. But M·A·C said they'd let me choose all the colors. When I told them I thought some of their lipsticks were too sheer, that they needed to be heavier, to contain more pigment, they

experimented in the laboratory and I was involved in the process. They also let me name the products in the collection, which had a bird theme, a nod to the *Rara Avis* show at the Costume Institute at the Metropolitan Museum of Art. The project was a staggering success. The lipsticks sold out online overnight. I was told that people were stealing the testers on display—how flattering!

I was photographed for the campaign by the great celebrity photographer Steven Klein, and I styled the image myself. Everything in the shot is mine, although the fabulous coat was on loan to me by my dear friend, Ralph Rucci, whose clothes I adore!

I'm the oldest living broad that ever graced a major cosmetics campaign.

Nothing makes a woman
look so old as trying desperately
hard to look young.

—COCO CHANEL

A woman is as old as she looks,
but a man is never old until
he stops looking.

—My grandfather, ABRAHAM ASOFSKY

Baby, you're the only one here
with your own face.

—My husband, CARL APFEL,
at a gala dinner

THERE'S
NOTHING
WRONG WITH
WRINKLES.

When you're older, trying to look years younger
is foolish, and you're not fooling anyone.
When you're seventy-five and you get a face-lift,
nobody's going to think you're thirty. If you have an
abnormality, or you were born with a nose like
Pinocchio, or if you've been in an accident, God
forbid, a plastic surgeon is a blessing. But to go
get work done or get injections to try to make
yourself look a few years younger is stupid.
And the results aren't permanent, either. Not to
mention the fact that something could go wrong;
you could end up looking like one of
Picasso's Cubist portraits.

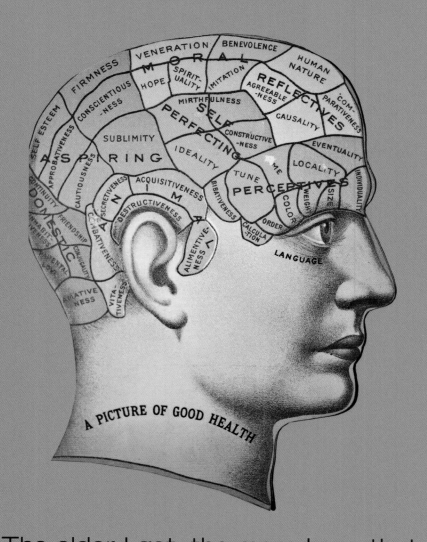

The older I get, the more I see that

COMMON SENSE
IS NOT
VERY COMMON.

USE YOUR
IMAGINATION

CREATIVITY IS A great emotional release; it keeps you happy and healthy.

You don't have to be an artist to be a creator, because creativity comes in a lot of forms, like cooking or keeping a house or dressing well. What you need is imagination, to make things up for yourself.

My family and I listened to the radio when I was young. I had to imagine the setting of the story and what the characters looked like during a radio show. That took creativity.

Unfortunately, creativity is suffering today because people now have an attention span of about twenty seconds. Art, fashion, and literature have all fallen victim to appropriation, with plenty of copycats riffing on the real McCoy and producing me-too designs.

I love what I do, which is to create. Besides, I have to work. People tell me I don't have to, but if I didn't work I'd never be able to get my creative urges out and it would make me sick.

I like to do different projects, like my jewelry line, Rara Avis by Iris Apfel for Home Shopping Network, which is sometimes based on my own vintage collection. When I'm peddling my creations on HSN, people call in and tell me I've made them think differently about dressing. It makes me happy to create attractive, unique accessories that are accessible to people of all income levels. Just because you can't afford or don't want to spend a lot of money on fashion doesn't mean you have to be deprived. I really feel that's my mission. A lot of women I've met in person say the same thing. If I have influenced them, I'd like to think it's in a positive way—following your instincts, taking risks.

The greatest luxury is
PEACE OF MIND.

I GET AN ENORMOUS HIGH FROM...

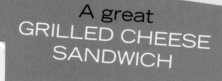
A great
GRILLED CHEESE
SANDWICH

Listening to
SINATRA'S
SALOON SONGS
in the wee hours

Any great rendition of
"LUSH LIFE"

Listening to
PEGGY LEE sing
"Is That All There Is"

Cruising a
FLEA MARKET

Reciting
"THE LOVE SONG OF
J. ALFRED PRUFROCK"
by T.S. Eliot. I know
it almost word for word.

CAVIAR,
my drug of
choice

A CHILLED TITO'S
HANDMADE VODKA
with a few drops of
Angostura Aromatic Bitters

Slipping into
A FRESHLY MADE BED
with crisp, clean sheets

Eating
STUFFED
CABBAGE

HOW TO LIVE
TO BE 200

I HAVE NO SECRETS to relay to you, dear reader, on the matter: the man upstairs has been very kind to me, and every year is another gift.

I never think about my age. Maybe that's the ticket. I never think about it—it's a passing thought. It's just a number,

Some people eat a lot of yogurt and live to be 127. Some people smoke twelve cigars and drink a bottle of booze every day and they're still out there, doing their thing. Everyone's got their story.

Abraham Lincoln once said, "In the end, it's not the years in your life that count. It's the life in your years." Keeping company with younger people is a good idea. They know what's going on—at least they *think* they do.

I've found that work is very healthy for me. I love what I do and I put my heart and soul into it. Since my husband died, I work even more to take my mind off his absence, which is good on one hand, but not so much on the other, when I push myself too hard.

It is true. Gettin' old ain't for sissies. You start falling apart, but you just have to buck up and paste yourself together. You may not like getting older, but what's the alternative? You're here—embrace it. I say put your experience to work, to give something back to other people.

That's one of the things I'm doing with the University of Texas at Austin, where I am a visiting professor. It's true—they even gave me my own business cards. Hoop Dee Doo!

That all started when Sue Meller, an alumna and close friend of the university saw *Rara Avis* at the Peabody Essex Museum. She went crazy over the show and called me. We spoke for a while, and then she asked me if I would be interested in creating an undergraduate program for the School of Human Ecology's Division of Textiles and Apparel. That sounded exciting, and I love an unusual challenge, so I agreed.

The school initially wanted me to introduce their students to designers and the fashion market, but I convinced them to expand their thinking, as I had just finished judging the designs of seniors' graduation projects from the major fashion schools in New York, and I was appalled at the students' lack of knowledge of the nonacademic fashion world. I told them that students needed to know that there are many other jobs other than designer or merchandiser. Fashion is a huge umbrella encompassing many areas, such as trend forecasting, licensing, archiving, styling, public relations, publishing, museum work, cosmetics, furs, jewelry, and so on. Interesting and lucrative jobs are available.

The school loved the idea but didn't know how to implement it.

"Why don't you do it?" they said.

Foolishly, I said yes without having a clue. I don't know how I did it. I just did it, pulling together a glorious amalgamation of talent.

The program, UT at NYC, began in 2011 and was an instant success. It exposes the students to a veritable Who's Who of the entire fashion-industry spectrum. As far as we know, it is the only university program of this scope with this caliber of executive and artistic talent in the industry in the United States, and it has become a valuable recruiting tool. The program has also been endowed in my name; this makes me really proud.

The students call it a life-changing experience. I'll admit, though, the itinerary can get very intense; we take the troupe to an average of four or five companies and institutions a day. I work very hard at it and am extremely grateful to my many friends in the industry for never turning me down. Their generosity to the program has been astounding. While many of the students have gotten excellent positions, their achievements have been my greatest reward.

You only have one trip, and the present is all you've got. The past isn't coming back, and the future isn't here yet! So live each day as though it were your last. And one day you'll be right.

LIFE IS A CELEBRATION!

There is definitely
no road map.
Embrace its glamour.
Enjoy its mystery.
Be open to the unexpected.
Stop asking why.
And remember that...

IN
WONDER
IT
ENDS.

ACKNOWLEDGMENTS

MANY WONDERFUL PEOPLE were part of the making of this opus.

I'd like to thank:

Inez Bailey, my extended family. Without her help and loving service for almost two decades, this book could never have happened. Her tender loving care for Carl is something I will never forget.

Juliet Brown, for her great care, patience, and love. Without her I couldn't have managed to do this complex project.

Elizabeth Viscott Sullivan, Executive Editor at Harper Design, for her creative vision, dedication, and passion; Lynne Yeamans, Paul Kepple, Max Vandenberg, Susan Kosko, and Dani Segelbaum for the crackerjack book design and production; Rebecca Karamehmedovic, for her ace image research; Matthew Wade Evans, for his assistance with the manuscript; Carmen Bruni, for her great kindness and for giving her time so freely; Barbara L. Dixon, for her help with fine-tuning the final text; Weegie Antle, for her kindness and support; Emerson Bruns, for his sage advice, unwavering gentility, and legal prowess; and John and Kim Wadsworth, for their generous assistance.

The illustrators Carlos Aponte, Bil Donovan, David Downton, Donald Robertson, Ruben Toledo, and Michael Vollbracht, for creating the artwork especially for the book—I am most honored.

The many talented artists and photographers who contributed their work: Alique, Eric Boman, Roger Davies, Daniela Federici, Eric Giriat, John Mark Hall, John Huba, Steven Klein, Robert Knoke, Dmitry Kostyukov, Harley Landberg, Keith Major, Luis Monteiro, Norman Nelson, Willy Soma, Nick Stocks, Emma Summerton, and Bruce Weber.

And finally, the many terrific companies I've had the pleasure of collaborating with over the years, with an additional bow to M•A•C, Macy's, Modern Kids, One Kings Lane, Neiman Marcus, and Tag Heuer for being so generous with their imagery.

PHOTOGRAPHY & ILLUSTRATION
CREDITS

HarperCollins books may be purchased for educational,
business, or sales promotional use. For information please
e-mail the Special Markets Department at
SPsales@harpercollins.com.

First published by
Harper Design
An Imprint of HarperCollinsPublishers
195 Broadway, New York, NY 10007
Tel: (212) 207-7000
Fax: (855) 746-6023
harperdesign@harpercollins.com
www.hc.com

Distributed throughout the world by
HarperCollinsPublishers
195 Broadway
New York, NY 10007

ISBN 978-0-06-240508-1

Library of Congress Control Number: 2016952333

Book design by Paul Kepple and Max Vandenberg
at Headcase Design

Printed in the United States Of America

First Printing, 2018

18 19 20 PC/WOR 5 4 3 2

ABOUT THE AUTHOR

IRIS BARREL APFEL is the World's Oldest Living Teenager. A renowned collector of and authority on antique textiles, she cofounded Old World Weavers, an international textile manufacturing company specializing in reproducing antique fabrics for an elite clientele. She was also a consultant to the White House during nine presidential administrations and produced fabric that still hangs in the Gold Room today. In 2005, the Costume Institute at the Metropolitan Museum of Art staged *Rara Avis*, a blockbuster exhibit of her clothing and accessories, making her the first living woman who was not a fashion designer to be so honored; the show then traveled to numerous other museum venues. Since that time she has been featured in many publications in print and online, and has collaborated with and been the face of an ever-growing list of brands and retailers worldwide. She sells Rara Avis, her line of clothing and accessories, on the Home Shopping Network. The subject of director Albert Maysles' award-winning feature film *Iris*, and a visiting professor at the University of Texas, she is the recipient of numerous awards, including a special award from the Women Together foundation at the United Nations.